SCHIRMER PERFORMANCE EDITIONS

HAL LEONARD PIANO LIBRARY

BEETHOVEN
FIVE FAVORITE PIANO SONATAS
Pathétique • Moonlight • The Tempest
Les Adieux • Op. 2, No. 1

T0039528

Edited by Robert Taub

The commentary on the sonatas has been excerpted and abridged from
Playing the Beethoven Piano Sonatas by Robert Taub,
published by Amadeus Press, distributed by Hal Leonard.

On the cover:
Sea beach in the fog
(1807)
by Caspar David Friedrich
(1774–1840)

ISBN 978-1-5400-1216-6

G. SCHIRMER, Inc.

DISTRIBUTED BY

7777 W. BLUEMOUND RD. P.O. BOX 13819 MILWAUKEE, WI 53213

www.musicsalesclassical.com
www.halleonard.com

CONTENTS

HISTORICAL NOTES

LUDWIG VAN BEETHOVEN (1770–1827)

THE PIANO SONATAS

In 1816, Beethoven wrote to his friend and admirer Carl Czerny: "You must forgive a composer who would rather hear his work just as he had written it, however beautifully you played it otherwise." Having lost patience with Czerny's excessive interpolations in the piano part of a performance of Beethoven's Quintet for Piano and Winds, Op. 16, Beethoven also addressed the envelope sarcastically to "Herr von Zerni, celebrated virtuoso." On all levels, Beethoven meant what he wrote.

As a composer who bridged the gulf between court and private patronage on one hand (the world of Bach, Handel, Haydn, and Mozart) and on the other hand earning a living based substantially on sales of printed works and/or public performances (the world of Brahms), Beethoven was one of the first composers to become almost obsessively concerned with the accuracy of his published scores. He often bemoaned the seeming unending streams of mistakes. "Fehler—fehler!—Sie sind selbst ein einziger Fehler" ("Mistakes—mistakes!—You yourselves are a unique mistake") he wrote to the august publishing firm of Breitkopf und Härtel in 1811.

It is not surprising, therefore, that toward the end of his life Beethoven twice (1822 and again in 1825) begged his publishers C.F. Peters and Schott to bring out a comprehensive complete edition of his works over which Beethoven himself would have editorial control, and would thus be able to ensure accuracy in all dimensions—notes, pedaling and fingering, expressive notations (dynamics, slurs), and articulations, and even movement headings. This never happened.

Beethoven was also obsessive about his musical sketches that he kept with him throughout his mature life. Desk sketchbooks, pocket sketchbooks: thousands of pages reveal his innermost compositional musings, his labored processes of creativity, the ideas that he abandoned, and the many others—often jumbled together—that he crafted through dint of extraordinary determination, single-minded purpose, and the inspiration of genius into works that endure all exigencies of time and place. In the autograph scores that Beethoven then sent on to publishers, further layers of the creative processes abound. But even these scores might not be the final word in a particular work; there are instances in which Beethoven made textual changes, additions, or deletions by way of letters to publishers, corrections to proofs, and/or post-publication changes to first editions.

We can appreciate the unique qualities of the Beethoven piano sonatas on many different levels. Beethoven's own relationship with these works was fundamentally different from his relationship to his works of other genres. The early sonatas served as vehicles for the young Beethoven as both composer and pianist forging his path in Vienna, the musical capital of Europe at that time. Throughout his compositional lifetime, even when he no longer performed publicly as a pianist, Beethoven used his thirty-two piano sonatas as crucibles for all manner of musical ideas, many of which he later re-crafted—often in a distilled or more rarefied manner—in the sixteen string quartets and the nine symphonies.

The pianoforte was evolving at an enormous rate during the last years of the eighteenth century extending through the first several decades of the nineteenth. As a leading pianist and musical figure of his day, Beethoven was in the vanguard of this technological development. He was not content to confine his often explosive playing to the smaller sonorous capabilities of the instruments he had on hand; similarly, his compositions demanded more from the pianofortes of the day—greater depth of sonority, more subtle levels of keyboard finesse and control, and increased registral range.

These sonatas themselves pushed forward further development and technical innovation from the piano manufacturers.

Motivating many of the sonatas are elements of extraordinary—even revolutionary—musical experimentation extending into domains of form, harmonic development, use of the instrument, and demands placed upon the performer, the piano, and the audience. However, the evolution of these works is not a simple straight line.

I believe that the usual chronological groupings of "early," "middle," and "late" are too superficial for Beethoven's piano sonatas. Since he composed more piano sonatas than substantial works of any other single genre (except songs) and the period of composition of the piano sonatas extends virtually throughout Beethoven's entire creative life, I prefer chronological groupings derived from more specific biographical and stylistic considerations. I delve into greater depth on this and other aspects of the sonatas in my book *Playing the Beethoven Piano Sonatas* (Amadeus Press).

1795–1800: Sonatas Op. 2, No. 1; Op. 2, No. 2; Op. 2, No. 3; Op. 7; Op. 10, No. 1; Op. 10, No. 2; Op. 10, No. 3; Op. 13; Op. 14, No. 1; Op. 14, No. 2; Op. 22; Op. 49, No. 1; Op. 49, No. 2

1800–1802: Sonatas Op. 26; Op. 27, No. 1; Op. 27, No. 2; Op. 28; Op. 31, No. 1; Op. 31, No. 2; Op. 31, No. 3

1804: Sonatas Op. 53, Op. 54, Op. 57

1809: Sonatas Op. 78, Op. 79, Op. 81a

1816–1822: Sonatas Op. 90, Op. 101, Op. 106, Op. 109, Op. 110, Op. 111

From 1804 (post-Heiligenstadt) forward, there were no more multiple sonata opus numbers; each work was assigned its own opus. Beethoven no longer played in public, and his relationship with the sonatas changed subtly.

—*Robert Taub*

PERFORMANCE NOTES

For the preparation of this edition, I have consulted autograph scores, first editions, and sketchbooks whenever possible. I have also read Beethoven's letters with particular attention to his many remarks concerning performances of his day and the lists of specific changes/corrections that he sent to publishers. We all know—as did Beethoven—that musical notation is imperfect, but it is the closest representation we have to the artistic ideal of a composer. We strive to represent that ideal as thoroughly and accurately as possible.

Tempo

My recordings of these sonatas are available for sale. I have also included my suggestions for tempo (metronome markings) for each sonata, at the beginning of each movement.

Fingering

I have included Beethoven's own fingering suggestions. His fingerings—intended not only for himself (in earlier sonatas) but primarily for successive generations of pianists—often reveal intensely musical intentions in their shaping of musical contour and molding of the hands to create specific musical textures. I have added my own fingering suggestions, all of which are aimed at creating meaningful musical constructs. As a general guide, I believe in minimizing hand motions as much as possible, and therefore many of my fingering suggestions are based on the pianist's hands proceeding in a straight line as long as musically viable and physically practicable. I also believe that the pianist can develop senses of tactile feeling for specific musical patterns.

Pedaling

I have also included Beethoven's pedal markings in this edition. These indications are integral parts of the musical fabric. However, since most often no pedal indication is offered, whenever necessary one should use the right pedal—sparingly and subtly—to help achieve *legato* playing as well as to enhance sonorities.

Ornamentation

My suggestions regarding ornamental turns concern the notion of keeping the contour smooth while providing an expressive musical gesture with an increased sense of forward direction. The actual starting note of a turn depends on the specific context: if it is preceded by the same note (as in Sonata Op. 10, No. 2, second movement, m. 42), then I would suggest that the turn is four notes, starting on the upper neighbor: upper neighbor, main note, lower neighbor, main note.

Sonata in F Major, Op. 10, No. 2:
second movement, m. 42, r.h.

However, if the turn is preceded by another note (as in Sonata Op. 10, No. 2, first movement, m. 38), then the turn could be five notes in total, starting on the main note: main note, upper neighbor, main note, lower neighbor, main note.

Sonata in F Major, Op. 10, No. 2:
first movement, m. 38, r.h.

Whenever Beethoven included an afterbeat (Nachschlag) for a trill, I have included it as well. When he did not, I have not added any.

Footnotes

Footnotes within the musical score offer contextual explanations and alternatives based on earlier representations of the music (first editions, autograph scores) that Beethoven had seen and corrected. In areas where specific markings are visible only in the autograph score, I explain the reasons and context for my choices of musical representation. Other footnotes are intended to clarify ways of playing specific ornaments.

Notes on the Individual Piano Sonatas[1]

PIANO SONATA NO. 1 IN F MINOR, OP. 2, NO. 1 (1795)

In autumn 1795, the twenty-five-year-old Beethoven played the three Sonatas Op. 2 for his former composition teacher Haydn, to whom they are dedicated, at a Friday morning concert at Prince Lichnowsky's (a great supporter of music in Vienna). Beethoven considered the three sonatas of Op. 2 illustrative of his ideals as a composer and pianist and worthy of publication, and they furthered his introduction into Viennese musical society.

The challenges of playing this piece begin with the first note of the **Allegro**. It has no phrase marking; it is not *staccato*, but neither is it *legato*, for it is not slurred to the following *staccato* notes. I play the opening C with more weight than the following *staccato* notes, but I make sure not to connect it in phrasing by separating it with a slight air space from the following F.

The use of dynamics is immediately striking—the first six measures build from *p* to *ff*, then fall away back to *p* by m. 8. The opening figure increases in intensity and corresponding sharpness of touch as it rises, and each time the turn at the end is played, it is also at a higher dynamic level.

Although the second theme is simply an inversion of the first, the entire musical feeling is different. The top line is now as *legato* as possible while the undulating left hand playing only E-flats now gives a feeling of instability. The *con espressione* marking that begins the ending of the exposition implies a slight lessening of the tempo. The C-flats here give a hint of E-flat minor; a weighty touch can help emphasize this subtlety.

Initially the dynamic in the development is *piano*. The *crescendos*, *fp* and *sf* markings, and the increased pace of harmonic change and increased registral range of the second theme (played in the bass beginning in m. 67) all generate greater intensity in this area of the piece. A clear sound, gradual increase of tension in the touch, and spare pedaling will allow the tensile strength of the counterpoint to prevail.

In observing the repeat sign for the second part of this movement, I maintain the tempo, saving the fermata over the last rest for the conclusion of the movement.

The first sixteen measures of the **Adagio** of Op. 2, No. 1 are a transcription of the second movement of a piano quartet (WoO 36) Beethoven had composed some ten years earlier. Clarity of lines is important in this movement. Textures are spare, and the general quality of sound is *dolce* (rather than the more syrupy *espressivo*).

The graceful **Menuetto** and the **Trio** remain in F (minor and major respectively). Both break with the pattern of eight-bar phrases, again postponing local cadences and thereby creating feelings of suspension. I believe that the dynamic contrasts in the second part of the Menuetto are sudden contrasts, not to be anticipated by *crescendos* or *decrescendos*. This is not merely a question of making one hand more prominent than the other but has more to do with qualities of voicing and sound, achieved by subtleties of touch and pedaling.

Beethoven used the term **Prestissimo** sparingly. When he wrote it, he meant it. Hence, the last movement of this sonata is played very fast indeed. The ubiquitous triplets at the beginning of this movement and the concentrated juxtaposition of dynamic extremes create an underpinning of urgency.

The middle section of this movement, marked *sempre piano e dolce*, provides an extraordinary contrast to the intensity of the first section. The music at the beginning of this area is structurally a transmutation of the music at the beginning of the sonata; the repeated left-hand chords and the rising right-hand arpeggio that begins the now aria-like theme hark back—perhaps subliminally for the listener but certainly consciously for the composer—to the material of the first movement.

Beethoven included repeat signs for both parts of the last movement, which allows the opportunity to play (and hear) the repetition of the music slightly differently from the way we hear it the first time through.

1 Excerpted from *Playing the Beethoven Piano Sonatas* by Robert Taub
edited and abridged by Susanne Sheston
© 2002 by Robert Taub
Published by Amadeus Press
Used by permission.

PIANO SONATA NO. 8 IN C MINOR, OP. 13
"Pathétique" (1798–99)

Beethoven himself designated the sobriquet "Pathétique," indicating that he fully intended for others to appreciate the dramatic content of Sonata Op. 13. Like his other two piano sonatas in C minor (Op. 10, No. 1 and Op. 111), the "Pathétique" is infused with extraordinary intensity.

The first marking of the **Grave** of Op. 13 is *fp*: what does it mean? How is it played? The idea is for the chord to be heard *forte* initially, then rapidly dying down to *piano*. This is fundamentally different from an accent within a *piano* context and from the *sforzando* marking first encountered here in m. 3. To achieve an effective *fp*, the pianist simply depresses the keys rapidly, creating the *forte*, then immediately allows them to rise so that the sound is damped almost instantaneously. Depressing the keys immediately once again so that the dampers rise quickly allows the strings to continue to vibrate but now with considerably less energy, *piano*. All this takes only a small fraction of a second but sets the stage for the drama that unfolds throughout the piece.

The tempo of the Grave is slow enough so that the sixty-fourth-note groupings are clear but not so slow as to be ponderous. The **Allegro molto e con brio** enters without interruption, and here, since the harmonic motion is basically slow, I play at the fastest tempo that allows for the bass tremolandos—which add mightily to the overall tension of the movement—to be transparent with only subtle pedaling. The touch on the *staccato* half notes (m. 15) is light, and the chords are separated but not sharply detached. I do not see any reason to slow down for the second theme (m. 51 on) but rather use a more singing tone and *legato* qualities of touch. I play all the mordents (m. 57 on) starting with the main note, on the beat.

In the development area, *crescendos* that were withheld from the ascending right-hand line in the exposition are present and give the impression that the line is pushing forward even though the tempo remains steady. For the first time (beginning in m. 150), the left hand has the melodic fragments under right-hand tremolandos, which should remain vibrant as they descend chromatically. Notably, the recapitulation does not include music from the opening Grave, but the coda does.

After the contrasts of tempo of the first movement and its interruptions of phrases, its *staccato* notes, and its inner tension; the long, singing phrases of the **Adagio cantabile** appear as welcome comfort. The movement is unabashedly lyrical with a three-tiered texture. Each line requires a different quality of sound, a different touch—flat fingers playing lightly for an accompaniment touch; slightly heavier, more rounded fingers for a singing tone.

Each of the two episodes concentrates on a different musical character. The stillness of the repeated bass and questioning character of the top line of the first episode contrast with the introspective, conversant qualities of the second. When the theme returns for the last time (m. 51) the accompaniment continues the triplet motion begun in the second episode, but it is important not to push the tempo ahead at this point and to maintain the repose of the character of the theme.

An interpretive decision for the **Rondo: Allegro** concerns its fundamental character. Is it tempestuous and headlong like the first movement, or is it more restrained, more held back? I believe the latter is the case. Although this movement is *alla breve*, I play it less fast than the first, at a speed that allows the lyricism of the top line to be felt in all its poignancy.

To preserve the tempo and for inner strength where the triplets begin (m. 33), I find a pulse of four beats per bar—rather than simply two—is helpful. Openness of tone—even within a dynamic of *piano*—is generally the rule in major key areas such as m. 44, in contrast to the soft intensity of the C minor theme.

PIANO SONATA NO. 14 IN C-SHARP MINOR, OP. 27, NO. 2 "Moonlight" (1801)

Although the first movement of this sonata may be among Beethoven's best-known piano compositions, the complete sonata, and particularly the anguished drama of the last movement, offers such a compelling artistic experience that I would hope that anyone who has played only the first movement would also become immersed in the rest of the work.

The character of the **Adagio sostenuto** is striking, with its gently veiled sonorities shifting subtly, wisps of melodic fragments floating above. The *alla breve* time signature implies a pulse of two beats per measure, even within Beethoven's designation of Adagio sostenuto, which guards against the music becoming lugubrious.

At the beginning of the movement, Beethoven included two indications for *senza sordini* (without dampers): *Si deve suonare tutto questo pezzo delicatissimamente e senza sordini* and *sempre pianissimo e senza sordini* (this whole piece ought to be played with the utmost delicacy and without dampers—and then—always very soft and without dampers). While I depress the pedal only slightly, just enough to raise the dampers off the strings to allow them to vibrate freely, the character of this movement requires the pedal to be changed discretely to avoid creating harmonic sludge. The *senza sordini* indication pertains to the entire first movement as a general approach to the quality of sound, similar to the initial *sempre pianissimo* indication.

The three-part texture that pervades this movement suggests different qualities of touch and sound for each different voice. The bass octaves are soft but deep, the undulating triplets are smooth and played with an accompaniment touch (flat, light fingers, not pressing too deeply into the keys), and the top line, although *pianissimo*, sings forth in a plaintive voice. In this Sonata *quasi una fantasia*, there is no second theme in the first movement—such were expectations stretched. The triplet accompaniment assumes a more melodic role and can be shaped accordingly as it is developed beginning in m. 32 on. Tension increases as new harmonies are explored, the bass remaining insistently on the G-sharp octave (the dominant) and the top line temporarily abandoned in favor of the searching qualities of the triplets.

In the short coda the portentous dotted rhythm is heard for the first time in the bass (but exclusively on G-sharps) as it exchanges registral placement with the triplets. The movement ends as quietly as it began. Beethoven wrote *Attacca subito il seguente*—an element of fantasia heard also in Op. 27, No. 1—and the second movement begins without any break in sound.

Despite the quicker pacing of the **Allegretto**, the mood is wistful and the textures delicate. The smooth lines of the Allegretto give way to *sforzando* syncopations in the **Trio**, a contrasting spot of good humor in this sonata. I like to voice the left-hand chords in mm. 45–48 first to the tenor and then to the bass upon the repeat, giving a slight weight to the chromatic lines. Although the Allegretto ends with a rest, I would think it very much in keeping with *quasi fantasia* to begin the third movement almost right away. Once again, an enharmonic change (this time from D-flat major back to C-sharp minor) is the pivot point.

This **Presto agitato** is the most extended of the three, and is the most overt dramatic center of the piece. I prefer a genuinely fast tempo; although the harmonic motion is not particularly rapid, finally the surface motion can be, and a feeling of agitation is generated from both speed and clarity. From the start, a three-part texture analogous to that of the first movement is established: the bass line is distinct, the upwardly climbing sixteenth-note figures are a general middle area, and the top register is reached with the punctuated eighth-note chords—*sforzando*, *staccato*, in pedal.

There are two fermatas, both over bare G-sharps, which is the dominant pitch and is hence fraught with expectations of resolution—one in m. 14 and the other in the parallel place in the recapitulation (m. 115). I hold these fermatas a long time. By creating feelings of suspense, seemingly spontaneously, they are crucial to the fantasia element, as is the four-measure cadenza-like passage in mm. 163–166, just four measures into the extended coda.

PIANO SONATA NO. 17 IN D MINOR, OP. 31, NO. 2 "The Tempest" (1801–02)

Sonata Op. 31, No. 2, "The Tempest," is a brooding work, starting from the opening rolled chord in the **Largo; Allegro**. The first six measures—improvisatory and concentrated—are not merely introductory but rather form a strong motivic and spiritual foundation for the remainder of the movement, and in fact, the entire sonata. The opening should create harmonic suspense, for the true harmonic setting of the first A major rolled chord is not yet defined. In m. 6, for the first time in the piece there is a sense of forward direction. With the left-hand six-four chord in m. 19 and the longest line in the right hand so far, a firm harmonic grounding begins to seem likely. I make the chromatic right hand smooth and the left-hand *sforzando* incisive, setting up the move to D minor in m. 21.

When we hear the largo measures after the exposition, we cannot know what follows. Three consecutive arpeggiations are a new idea, but the arpeggiations span a greater registral range here. Since they are not rolled chords, I play them slower and with more questioning feelings than the opening largo measures. The fermatas on the last note of each are held a long time, but the rests following the first two are strictly in tempo. Only the last note of this chain—the A-sharp—is held directly into the next measure with no break in sound. I tend to hold this last fermata the longest of the three, for the surprise explosive return of the main theme in F-sharp minor is the first *fortissimo* of the movement.

When the A-major arpeggiation of the opening finally recurs, the prolongation of the expected home key is a pivotal factor in the extraordinary recitative that follows. Changing the pedal indication within this phrase (Beethoven's own), as unusual to us as the pedal marking might initially seem, destroys the line of the music.

The **Adagio** begins also with a rolled chord, but this time it is a stable, root-position chord. Accordingly, I play it with more of a definite feeling, rolled straight to the top, no hesitancy or coming away from the bottom note as in the initial rolled chord of the first movement. The division of the theme into two registers—as first encountered in the main theme of the Allegro—is reversed here, with the top line answered by the lower chords. The touch here is open, singing, and relaxed, opposite to that of the entire first movement. Recurring left-hand thirty-second-note triplets can help build intensity with touch and dynamics when the music suggests, such as in the *crescendos* beginning in m. 24 and in m. 39.

When the main theme recurs in m. 50, I try to make the left-hand embellished accompaniment as light and fluid as possible. The left hand plays over the right, with flat fingers and light pedaling. A particularly dramatic moment is the solo left-hand bass B-flat making a *crescendo* to the low A, *piano subito*, in mm. 91–92. The bare A should not be rushed; when allowed to resonate for a full measure it suggests a darker harmonic image, one that may possibly return to D minor. In the final measure, there is no fermata; the music ends quietly.

The **Allegretto** sonata-form last movement is obsessive in its use of the arpeggiated chord, but in a thoroughly composed rather than stylistically improvisatory manner. As suggested by the careful voicing of the left hand, I give a slight extra stress to the sustained offbeat A's. This helps destabilize the tonic somewhat. The right hand is gentle, and I think it's important to maintain a pulse of three eighth notes per bar, rather than allowing the music to lapse into a single beat per measure.

I pedal lightly in the last three measures of the movement so that the arpeggio gathers in sonority only gradually, allowing the last D—finally root position—to be the most final.

PIANO SONATA NO. 26 IN E-FLAT MAJOR, OP. 81A "Les Adieux" ("Das Lebewohl") (1809)

Beethoven dedicated Sonata Op. 81a ("Das Lebewohl", as he preferred) to his friend and patron, Archduke Rudolph. The sonata's three movements portray the leave-taking, the absence, and the return of the archduke during the Napoleonic invasion of Vienna in 1809. The only one of Beethoven's sonatas to embody an extramusical program, the events it portrays are central to its interpretation.

The opening **Adagio** introduces the motive (over which Beethoven wrote *Le-be-wohl*) with a sense of intimacy, *piano* and *espressivo*. Although the first measure of the joyful Allegro is in a new, fast tempo, I hold the first chord of m. 18 just a little longer than the beat would ordinarily be, as implied by the *tenuto* indication above it. I also try to play the left-hand chromatic descent clearly, giving an added dimension of strength to the music. When eighth notes are played beginning in m. 21, the left hand becomes lighter, but the right hand continues its *crescendo* up to the top B-flat octave, before which I like to wait just a tiny fraction of a second, postponing the *sforzando* with an imperial gesture.

The "Lebewohl" motive is the melodic basis for most of the development area, as it is played in a wide range of different harmonic settings as if the music is searching for just the right path to continue. The leave-taking becomes understandably more prolonged with the motive's repetition in its barest form beginning in m. 223, but the tempo remains steady. I take a little extra time on the poignant high C appoggiaturas in mm. 248 and 250, the final questioning phrases of this movement before the final *crescendo* beginning with the octave C's (m. 252) ensures that the movement finishes strongly, in tempo.

The second movement—"**Abwesenheit**" (absence) —is not a slow, songful Adagio but rather a restless Andante espressivo. In mm. 13 and 14, as the musical line takes flight, I still maintain a pulse of four to the measure, increasing the weight of touch with the *portato* marking at the end of m. 14 and playing with a decidedly more singing tone as the *legato* line enters in m. 15. An altogether different quality of sound, one more mysterious and intense, is invoked by the subtle use of the right pedal in mm. 37 and 39. As with such markings earlier, I depress the pedal not fully to the floor but just enough to raise the dampers off the strings, allowing them to vibrate freely for the duration of the pedal marking.

I know of no greater outpouring of musical exuberance than the first ten bars of the third movement, "**Wiedersehen**" (return). These measures are extremely brilliant and virtuosic. Following the first chord, I drop in dynamic only to let it rise again as the line does. The *diminuendo* in m. 5 continues until the *forte subito* in m. 9, and once again, I drop to a lower dynamic level to start the rising line, which I play without slowing down, with increasing intensity in touch and dynamics.

Even the quieter second theme is brilliant in its extroversion. *Crescendos* and *decrescendos* are shaped by the inside measured trills beginning in m. 53. When the right hand plays off the beat (m. 69 on), I make sure not to pedal too heavily, so that the left hand remains clear and the main beats are not lost in a mass of too much sound.

The coda is marked *poco andante*, which I interpret to mean that each eighth note of the 6/8 meter is heard at a walking tempo. The pace really is quite a bit slower, considering that the body of the movement is at a most lively tempo. I like to consider the beginning of this coda as quasi-improvisatory, and I allow the pulse to be quite flexible. The final flourish leads to an emphatic cadence.

Final Thoughts

Beethoven's sonatas—as individual works, or taken together as a complete cycle—are pieces that we can listen to, learn, play, put away, relearn, and perform again over and over—with only increasing joy, involvement, and meaning. For those of you looking at the musical score as you follow a recording, welcome. For those playing these pieces for the first time, I invite you to become involved. And for those returning to these sonatas after learning them previously—or comparing this edition to any other—I invite you to roll up your sleeves and start playing, for there is always more to do. The expressive universe conjured up by the Beethoven piano sonatas is unprecedented, and unequalled.

—*Robert Taub*

References

For sources consulted in researching this edition, please see the Bibliography in *Playing the Beethoven Piano Sonatas*, by Robert Taub, published by Amadeus Press (Hal Leonard).

Dedicated to Joseph Haydn

Sonata in F minor

Opus 2 no. 1
Composed in 1795

a) The fingering in italics is Beethoven's. b) short appoggiatura, played before the beat   c)

d) The Artaria first edition (1796) and Simrock (1798) include repetition signs for the second part of this movement.

e) D-flat, not D-natural   f)

Adagio (♩ = 72)

g) h) i) j) as in g) k) G-sharp also in Artaria; in Lischke, simply ∿

MENUETTO
Allegretto (♩ = 144)

p) Played as a short appoggiatura: ![notation] in contrast to the written-out long appoggiatura in mm. 22 and 23.

Menuetto D.C.

q) without tail

Dedicated to Prince Carl von Lichnowsky

Sonata in C minor
(Pathétique)

Opus 13
Composed in 1798–99

8.

a) three triplets b) two triplets c) play evenly; no sub-division

Attacca subito l'Allegro:

Allegro molto e con brio ($\d = 152$)

d) as in the first edition; subsequent editions have   e) LH over RH   f) short appoggiatura

g) as in the first edition; subsequent editions have

Adagio cantabile ($\flat$ = 66)

h) $\widehat{3\,4}$ first, then $\widehat{1\,2}$ i)

RONDO
Allegro (♩ = 84)

j)   k) short appoggiatura

Dedicated to Countess Giulietta Guicciardi

Sonata in C-sharp minor
(Sonata quasi una Fantasia)
"Moonlight"

Opus 27 no. 2
Composed in 1801

Adagio sostenuto (♩ = 30 or ♪ = 60)

Si deve suonare tutto questo pezzo delicatissimamente e senza sordini.

14.

a) *sempre pianissimo e senza sordini*

a) The pedal indication (senza sordini—without dampers) is Beethoven's.

Attacca subito il seguente

Allegretto (♩.= 63)
La prima parte senza repetizione

Fine

TRIO

Allegretto da capo

Presto agitato ($\bullet$ = 88)

b) As per autograph score: "normal" pedaling in mm. 163–164; one long pedal in mm. 165–166; "normal" again in m. 167.

Sonata in D minor

Opus 31 no. 2
Composed in 1801–02

a) The fingering in italics and the pedal markings are Beethoven's.

b) l.h. over r.h.

c) Pedal off on fourth beat (with the ♩); same for m. 96

d) The D-flat on the final sixteenth-note in the first edition is a printer's error. In a copy owned by the Gesellschaft der Musikfreunde, it has been corrected by Beethoven to C.

g) with tail   h) with tail

Allegretto[♩. = 69]

Upon the Departure of Archduke Rudolph, Vienna, 4th May 1809

Sonata in E-flat Major

Ludwig van Beethoven
Opus 81a
Composed in 1809

attacca subito l'Allegro

a) Despite Beethoven's expressly stated title "Das Lebewohl," the first edition is entitled "Sonate caractéristique: Les adieux, l'absence, et le retour." This misrepresentation was often criticized by Beethoven. b) The fingering in italics and the pedal markings are Beethoven's.

c) In the autograph score, a **p** in this measure replaces an erased $>$; hence the parentheses around the **p** in m. 94.

d) The legato slur here is in accordance with the autograph manuscript and first edition, and contrasts with the slurs in mm. 23–24. e) The LH passage is in accordance with the autograph manuscript and first edition, and contrasts with the parallel passage in m. 25.

f) The autograph includes a D in this chord; early editions do not.

ABWESENHEIT
Andante espressivo (♪ = 69)
In gehender Bewegung, doch mit Ausdruck

g) The low E was not present in Beethoven's fortepiano at this time. Only with Sonata Op. 101 did Beethoven first use this note in a piano work, since fortepianos of 1816 included it.

WIEDERSEHEN
Vivacissimamente (♩. = 112)
Im lebhaftesten Zeitmaasse

Im Januar 1810

h) without tail

ABOUT THE EDITOR

ROBERT TAUB

From New York's Carnegie Hall to Hong Kong's Cultural Centre to Germany's *avant garde* Zentrum für Kunst und Medientechnologie, Robert Taub is acclaimed internationally. He has performed as soloist with the MET Orchestra in Carnegie Hall, the Boston Symphony Orchestra, BBC Philharmonic, The Philadelphia Orchestra, San Francisco Symphony, Los Angeles Philharmonic, Montreal Symphony, Munich Philharmonic, Orchestra of St. Luke's, Hong Kong Philharmonic, Singapore Symphony, and others.

Robert Taub has performed solo recitals on the Great Performers Series at New York's Lincoln Center and other major series worldwide. He has been featured in international festivals, including the Saratoga Festival, the Lichfield Festival in England, San Francisco's Midsummer Mozart Festival, the Geneva International Summer Festival, among others.

Following the conclusion of his highly celebrated New York series of Beethoven Piano Sonatas, Taub completed a sold-out Beethoven cycle in London at Hampton Court Palace. His recordings of the complete Beethoven Piano Sonatas have been praised throughout the world for their insight, freshness, and emotional involvement. In addition to performing, Robert Taub is an eloquent spokesman for music, giving frequent engaging and informal lectures and pre-concert talks. His book on Beethoven—*Playing the Beethoven Piano Sonatas*—has been published internationally by Amadeus Press.

Taub was featured in a recent PBS television program—*Big Ideas*—that highlighted him playing and discussing Beethoven Piano Sonatas. Filmed during his time as Artist-in-Residence at the Institute for Advanced Study, this program has been broadcast throughout the US on PBS affiliates.

Robert Taub's performances are frequently broadcast on radio networks around the world, including the NPR (Performance Today), Ireland's RTE, and Hong Kong's RTHK. He has also recorded the Sonatas of Scriabin and works of Beethoven, Schumann, Liszt, and Babbitt for Harmonia Mundi, several of which have been selected as "critic's favorites" by *Gramophone*, *Newsweek*, *The New York Times*, *The Washington Post*, *Ovation*, and *Fanfare*.

Robert Taub is involved with contemporary music as well as the established literature, premiering piano concertos by Milton Babbitt (MET Orchestra, James Levine) and Mel Powell (Los Angeles Philharmonic), and making the first recordings of the Persichetti Piano Concerto (Philadelphia Orchestra, Charles Dutoit) and Sessions Piano Concerto. He has premiered six works of Milton Babbitt (solo piano, chamber music, Second Piano Concerto). Taub has also collaborated with several 21st-century composers, including Jonathan Dawe (USA), David Bessell (UK), and Ludger Brümmer (Germany) performing their works in America and Europe.

Taub is a Phi Beta Kappa graduate of Princeton where he was a University Scholar. As a Danforth Fellow he completed his doctoral degree at The Juilliard School where he received the highest award in piano. Taub has served as Artist-in-Residence at Harvard University, at UC Davis, as well as at the Institute for Advanced Study. He has led music forums at Oxford and Cambridge Universities and The Juilliard School. Taub has also been Visiting Professor at Princeton University and at Kingston University (UK).